THE SMART PLAYBOOK™
Game-changing life skills for a modern world

Suzanne M. Wind

Copyright © 2014 by Suzanne M. Wind

All rights reserved. This book or any portion thereof may not be reproduced or used in any manner whatsoever without the express written permission of the publisher except for the use of a brief questions in a book review or scholarly journal.

First Printing 2014

ISBN-13: 978-1495935275

ISBN-10: 1495935272

ModernGrace Publishing
Greenwich, CT

thesmartplaybook@gmail.com
www.thesmartplaybook.com

Order Information: Special discounts are available on quantity purchase by corporation, associations, educators and others. For details contact the publisher at the above email address.

SMART
PRAISE AND AWARDS

The Mom's Choice Awards® among the best in family-friendly media, products and services at the highest - gold - level.

Honored with the distinguished **Creative Child Magazine 2014 Book of the Year** Award, one of today's foremost children's education publications.

Multiple Awards from **The Toy Man® News and Reviews** - a highly recognized international leader in independent product and service evaluation:

- The Toy Man® "Award of Excellence"
- The Toy Man® S.T.E.M Award
- The Toy Man® eChoice Award
- The Toy Man® "Mom-Approved - Comme Il Faut" Award

Proud Recipient of 7 Prestigious Awards!

Recognized with the **Mr. Dad Seal of Approval**, an endorsement that carries the powerful credibility of Americans leading authority on successful fatherhood.

"I TRULY love the whole concept. Parents can make sure their children develop vital social skills while having a fun experience with kids. The information is helpful and the tone is pitch-perfect."

— **Dr. Andrea Archibald,** *Child Psychologist and Chief Girl Expert for Girls Scouts of USA*

"As we all know, most of the very important life lessons are learned at home. This workbook is a great 'family project' to help teach and reinforce vital life skills - fun and social skill building all-in-one."

— **Anita Kulick,** *President & CEO, Educating Communities for Parenting*

"...this is where the fantastic book **The SMART Playbook** by Suzanne M Wind comes into play, quite literally This book's curriculum teaches your child or students real life manners and practical skills in a very relatable and child friendly format."

— **Jill R.** *@ Enchanted Homeschooling Mom*

"...a practical guide to building social skills in a fun and engaging format. A great tool to help children and their families."

— **Dr. Karen Beckman,** *Riverside Pediatrics*

DEDICATION & ACKNOWLEDGEMENTS:

This book is dedicated to my family. To my mormor and morfar, the two most socially graceful people I've ever known. To my mom and dad who raised me with an appreciation for manners—always reminding me to respect life's little unwritten rules. Thank you to my sons Charlie & Nicky, whom I credit for the sports theme and the stick figures. And to my little Annie who inspired the crown to top it off. Finally, I love you Chad—thanks for believing in The SMART Playbook every day.

CONTENTS

- A WORD TO THE COACHES (That means you, parents!) 01
- PLAYER INTRODUCTION 03
- THE SMART CONTRACT 04
- LET THE GAMES BEGIN 05
- GAME PLAN #2 – MEALTIME MANNERS 07
    - a) Table Setting 101
    - b) Pre-Dinner Prep
    - c) Utensils @ Play
    - d) The Winning Play Review
    - e) Let's Practice
    - f) Answers
    - g) Ticket Tally Score Board

- EXTRA BONUS 37
- AWARD CEREMONY 47

⇨ A WORD TO THE COACHES (That Means You, Parents!)

The SMART Playbook was founded by a mom of three, with a possibly impossible mission: to offer families a simple and effective game plan to teach relevant life skills for a modern world. Teaching social skills and manners in this fast-paced, tech-focused society is easier said than done. How do we get our kids back to basics without overwhelming our time?

THE SOLUTION: The SMART Playbook. Written in a relatable style and chock full of games, The SMART Playbook will lead you and your child in a collaborative effort to bring manners to a new generation. Your child is the player, the book is the guide, and you are the coach. Life is the referee.

5 SMART topics to help your child succeed in life!
(The topic in this book is in the arrow.)

- ✣ Social Skill Basics — The principles of modern manners

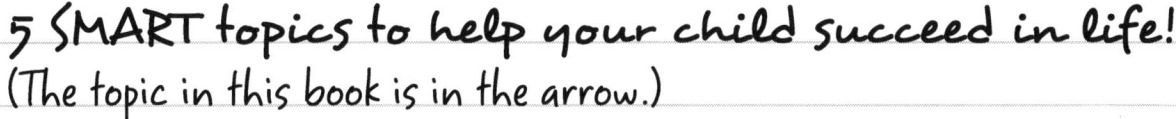
- ✣ Mealtime Manners — A guide to mealtime etiquette

- ✣ Art of Conversation — Eloquent face-to-face conversational skills
- ✣ Restaurant Behavior — The finer points of restaurant conduct
- ✣ Technology Talk — Internet safety and responsible usage

THE BENEFIT: The methods included in The SMART Playbook will help your child gain confidence, character, integrity and empathy in face-to-face situations and technology usage.

HOW TO USE: Fill out the SMART contract. (This will help motivate your child to complete the lessons.) As your child completes game challenges, he or she earns tickets and you decide the prizes. As the coach, your job is to encourage your child to work on the lessons and take the challenges. When you play the family scrimmage games, reward your child with lots of tickets!

THE RESULT: A happy and confident child thriving in a modern world.

⇨ PLAYER INTRODUCTION

Dear Player,
Getting older is awesome, but there's also more expected of you. If you know the guidelines for interacting with people, growing up is so much easier.

Social skills and manners are the keys to having great friends, gaining respect from adults and growing your self-confidence. Wouldn't it be great to know the ins and outs of all the rules to guide you?

The SMART Playbook lets you in on commonsense guidelines. Through games and challenges you will learn how to handle all sorts of new situations both in person and while using technology. And to top it off, you will look like a star player!

Have a great time playing, and best of luck!

From,
Suzanne Wind, the author of The SMART Playbook

Ready to get in the game yet?
Accept the challenge? Fill out the SMART Contract on the next page. Then move on to earn tickets and win prizes. **Ready, Set, Go!**

THE SMART CONTRACT

This is an agreement between you and your parents. Here's your chance to ask for a cool prize in exchange for learning game-changing life skills. It's a win-win situation.

What's a win-win situation, you might ask? It means you earn something super-cool (and of your own choosing!) by simply learning life rules and plays. **Please fill this out before you begin.**

Date: _____

I _____ agree to carefully read and complete The SMART Playbook.

1) I promise to share one fact every time I learn something new with the rest of the family.

2) I promise to share many games and activities so that my family can practice modern manners together.

3) Each time I finish a game challenge I'll earn a ticket. My parents promise to reward me with the following (Make sure to determine how many tickets you need to win!):

_____
_____
_____
_____

4) After completing this entire playbook, (besides being a Star Player) my parents agree to reward me with the following:

_____
_____
_____
_____

Good Luck Playing!

_____   _____
Player Signature   Coach Signature

▷ LET THE GAMES BEGIN!

THE GOAL:

Learn and use modern manners and social skills to help you get along with all people and make you feel more confident. Think of it this way: there are set rules in sports to ensure fair play and to give everyone an equal chance to win. Practice and dedication makes you a great athlete.

Practice and dedication helps you learn SMART plays and wins you the Golden ticket to being your best in life.

Life Skills Required:
The playbook is divided into five SMART game sections: Social Skill Basics, Mealtime Manners, Art of Conversation, Restaurant Behavior and Technology Talk.

Equipment Needed:

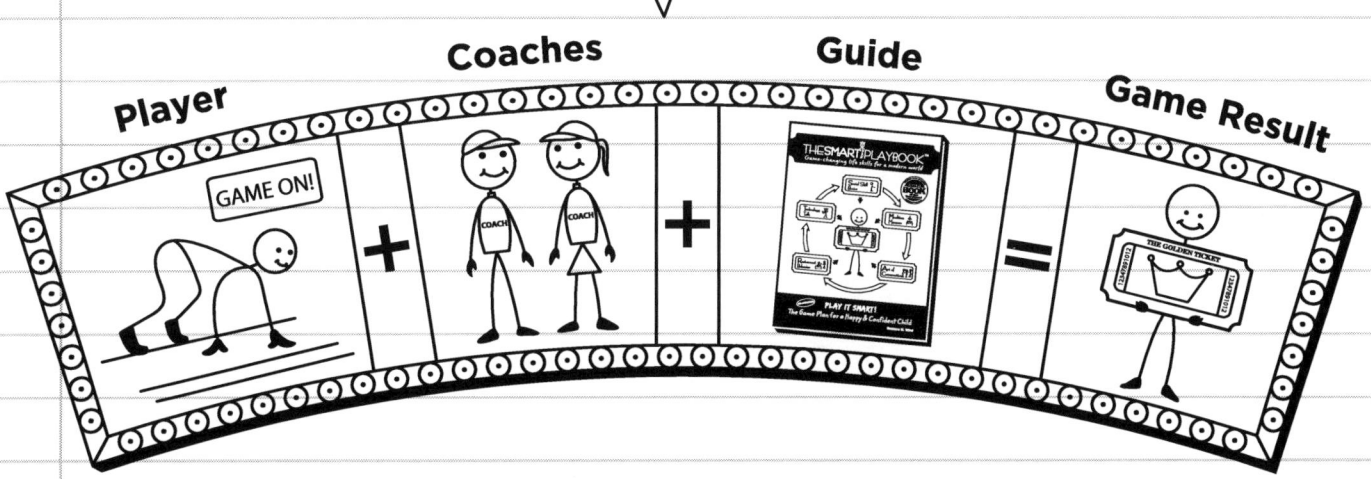

Player + Coaches + Guide = Game Result

GAME PLAN #2 - MEALTIME MANNERS

GOAL:

Have you ever seen pigs eat at the farm? The farmer pours the food down and the pigs all swarm the food in a feeding frenzy. They will grab, push, snort and gulp down as much food as possible.

You might be in a hurry to get to a game or super hungry after a long day at school, but don't forget your manners at the table. Mealtime should be an enjoyable moment with friends and family. Let's all be on the same playing field and learn table manners.

Life Skills Required:
- Table Setting 101
- Pre-Dinner Prep
- Utensils @ Play
- Eating Rules
- Finish Line

Equipment needed:
- You
- Parents, siblings and friends to practice
- Utensils, tableware and food

Game Directions:
- Take the challenges
- Have an adult check the box at the end of the game after you complete the challenge
- Cash in your tickets for the reward chosen with your coach (your parents)

Ticket Goal:_____
Game Prize:_____

S M A R T

TABLE SETTING 101

A pretty placemat. A nice table setting. A flower arrangement in the middle. The way you set the table can change the appearance of the food and sets the tone of the meal. At your house, you will most likely use a basic casual table setting for every day eating. When you attend formal holiday events and visit restaurants, you will see more formal settings.

ARRANGE FLATWARE AROUND PLATE IN THE ORDER THAT IT IS USED!

You set the table with what is needed for the meal. Flatware (your utensils) is arranged around a main plate in the order that it is used-starting at the outside and working towards the center (the main plate).

The Players and Positions

In this game, it's the utensils who are the players! Their positions and roles are detailed here.

> The first eating utensil consisted of simple sharp stones to cut meat and fruit. Spoons were made from hollow pieces of wood or seashells and connected to a stick. Animal horns were also used to drink liquids.

THE BASIC GAME PLAN

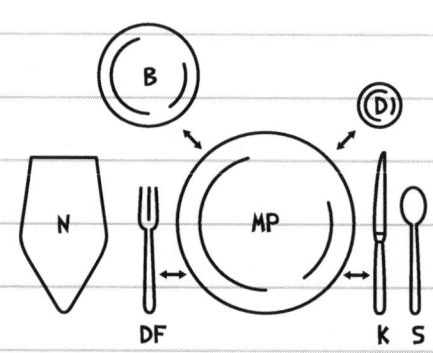

↔ **1 inch spaces between arrow positions!

08

The Main Plate (MP)

The plate is the main and most valuable player (MP). Everything will focus around the MP.

> Everything revolves around the MAIN PLATE - MP.

He is center stage on the field with players on all sides. Sometimes there is a saved spot for him and sometimes he makes a grand entrance! In more formal settings, he might have the napkin join him in the center.

The Bread Plate (b)

The bread plate (b) has a side role about 1 inch diagonally next to MP. He is a supporting player for your bread. His position is on the top left side of MP. He is not always around for every meal.

The Drink Glass (d)

The drink glass (d) has a side role place on the right side ◎ one inch diagonally from MP and above the knife.

TIME OUT!
Knock, Knock!
-Who's there?
Dishes
-Dishes who?
Dishes me, who are you?

The Fork (DF)
The fork has a handle and the top part are the prongs. There are different type of forks. The most important fork is the dinner fork (DF). The DF is always placed about one inch away from the MP on the left side.

The Knife (K)
The dinner knife is another supporting player during the meal. It has a good position on the right side about one inch away from MP. The blade faces the plate. If the main course requires a steak knife (a sharper knife), it becomes the substitute player for the dinner knife.

The Spoon (S)
The soup spoon is a reserve player only used when you are having soup. It takes the position next to the Knife (K). In a more formal setting you may have a dessert spoon on the top.

TIME OUT!
Q: What did one knife say to another?
A: You look sharp!

Additions to the Roster
Now that we understand the basic players and their positions, let's add some players to create a more formal table setting.
The players include a salad fork, a dessert spoon and fork and a wine glass.

Table Setting Tricks

There's a bag of tricks for learning how to set a table and what to use first! The tried-and true-tricks:

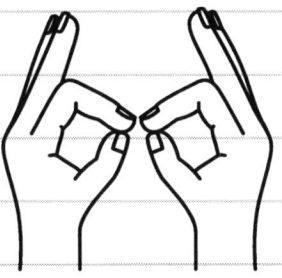

Letters b and d
Hold your hands in front of you. Touch the tips of your thumbs to the tips of your forefingers to create an 'o'. Use your left hand to make a lower case 'b'. The bread plate goes on the left side. Use your right hand to make a lower case 'd' to remind you that drinks go on the right.

Whose team are you on?
✣ Most of the items that are spelled with four letters will be to your left (L-E-F-T)
F-O-R-K, R-O-L-L
✣ Most of the items that are spelled with five letters will be on your right (R-I-G-H-T)
K-N-I-F-E, S-P-O-O-N, D-R-I-N-K

> TABLE SETTING TRICKS: THE b & d. WHOSE TEAM ARE YOU ON AND HOW FORKS CAN HELP YOU!

The word FORKS (minus the R)
The order left to right F is for fork, O for plate, K for knives, and S for spoons.

GAME CHALLENGE #1: Name 5 things that are wrong with this basic table setting:

1.
2.
3.
4.
5.

PRE-DINNER PREP

Pre-game skills prepare you for a great match! You put on your uniform, tie your shoes and warm up, and sometimes say the "Pledge of Allegiance" or sing the national anthem. Just like sports, there are rules to follow before we eat.

Basic Dress Code

> BEFORE YOU EAT, WASH YOUR HANDS AND DRESS APPROPRIATELY.

First wash your hands and dress appropriately. If you are eating inside at a table you should wear a shirt and take off your cap or hat. If your clothes are dirty, you should change them before sitting down. Obviously if you are at the beach, a casual BBQ, or a pool party you will have a different set of rules.

> WAIT TO EAT UNTIL EVERYONE IS SEATED! FOLLOW YOUR HOST.

Wait for the Signal...

Once you are seated, you should wait until everyone is served and the hostess (often your parents) sits down. It's always nice to begin by thanking the cook. "Thanks mom (or dad), the dinner looks really good." In some homes, you say grace before you eat. If you are invited to dine with a family that says grace, but it is not something you do at home, just politely bow your head and listen. Begin eating once you get a signal from a grown up.

RULE BREAKERS!

- DON'T have dirty hands at the table.
- DON'T sit down and start eating before everyone is seated.
- DON'T wear caps or hats at the table.

GAME CHALLENGE #2: True or False? You should wait for everyone to be seated before beginning your meal.

Sitting Position

At the dinner table, sit up straight (even if you are tired or sick!). And never put your elbows on the table while eating. Once you are seated, stay seated quietly without squirming or rocking.

RULE BREAKERS!

- DON'T have 'ants in your pants' at dinner. No moving around and getting up during dinner.
- DON'T play with your food or your utensils, plates, bowls and cups.

> SIT STILL. USE GOOD POSTURE AND NO ELBOWS ON TABLE. PLEASE!

The Napkin

Is it a towel? A new shirt? What is the purpose of the napkin? Before eating, the napkin should be placed on your lap and used throughout the meal. Use a gentle tap or dab to remove any bits of food that didn't quite make it into the mouth. Then place your napkin back down on your lap. If you need to leave the table during dinner, leave it on your chair. And when finished, place the napkin in the empty spot where the plate used to be or on the side.

> PLACE THE NAPKIN ON YOUR LAP AND USE IT TO DAB ANY STRAY BITS OF FOOD.

RULE BREAKERS!

- Don't start eating before the napkin is in your lap.
- Don't use your sleeve or the tablecloth to replace the napkin.
- Don't lick your fingers to wipe off food.
- Don't wave the napkin in the air and attach it to yourself as a bib.
- Don't use the napkin as a washcloth on your face.

SMART

UTENSILS @ PLAY

Using utensils can be compared to riding a bike. If your balance is off, it won't work very well. Food won't launch off the table or spill onto your clothes if you use utensils correctly. Don't worry—it takes practice and patience!

TOP UTENSIL USAGE Plays:

- Use utensils on the outside first and work your way inward with each new course that is served.
- If you are not sure which utensil to use, wait to see what is served.
- Watch others at the table and follow their lead.

> WHEN USING UTENSILS FOLLOW THE OUTSIDE-IN RULE. OUTSIDE FIRST AND THEN WORK YOUR WAY INWARD.

The Grip Technique

Place utensils in your palms

> In the old days, children had to learn to hold down their elbows using a book. They had to carefully cut their food and hold down their elbows to not drop the book.

Hold out your hand and gently place the utensils in the palm of your hand. For all right-handed users, the fork should remain in the left hand and the knife is in the right hand. For all left-handed users reverse the hands. Notice that the prongs will be facing up when you place it in your palm. And the knife blade will be facing the other palm.

Turn your hands over

Place and keep the index finger (point the index finger) on the back of the fork and knife and then turn your palm and utensils over. The knife is in your right hand. The index finger is straight and rests near the base of the top. The sharp side is down. The other four fingers then wrap around the handle. The fork is in your left hand. The prongs face downward from you. The index finger is straight and rests on the back-side

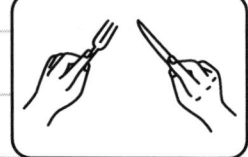

near the head of the fork. The other four fingers wrap around the handle.

> **GAME CHALLENGE #3:** What's the difference between a salad fork and a regular fork?

Cutting

Once you have mastered the grip, it's time to move on to cutting.

Apply sufficient pressure

Hold the food with the fork by applying pressure to the index finger. Cut with the knife, in the same way. Keep just a little pressure to the top of the utensils while you cut.

> HOLD THE KNIFE AND FORK CORRECTLY TO CUT WITH EASE.

Move the knife back and forth to cut.

Apply a little bit more pressure if it's difficult to cut. Make sure to keep your elbows down!

Cut a bite size piece before eating.

Take small bites even if you are hungry or the food is difficult to cut. If it is too hard to cut, just ask a grown up for help.

With small items like rice or beans you can turn the fork over and use a scooping style. Use your knife to help scoop the pieces. Don't use your fingers as little helpers. The knife is a much better player!

RULE BREAKERS!

- DON'T hold utensils like a shovel.
- DON'T get puffy cheeks from placing too much food in your mouth.
- DON'T use your fingers or hands unless it's a finger food.
- DON'T wave your utensils around in the air.
- DON'T talk with your mouth open. No one wants to see what is inside of he mouth!
- DON"T cut the entire chicken before eating. Cut small pieces to eat one piece at a time.

Eating Styles

> **CHOOSE YOUR EATING STYLE:** American or Continental?

What do you do after you have finished cutting? Choose your eating style—the American style or the Continental style (also known as European style).

American Style

Three steps: 1. Cut. 2. Switch hands. 3. Eat.

Fork starts in the left hand while you cut. Then put down the knife and switch the fork to the opposite hand to eat. Let's call this play Criss Cross, Pass & Touchdown.

Continental style

Two steps: 1. Cut and 2. Eat.

Fork in the left hand and knife in the right hand. You cut and eat the food in this position. There is no switching hands. Let's call this play Zig Zag & Score.

Resting & Finished Positions

> **TWO SECRET CODES:** resting and finished positions for the utensils.

Just like sports, there are secret codes in the game of table manners. These codes let people know if you are resting or finished with your meal.

The Backward "V" Sign

Rest your utensils on the plate in a backward "V" to show that you are still eating. Never rest utensils on the table or the linens. This sign is often used when you eat using the Continental style. Or if you need a rest while cutting food.

'Time Out' American Style
Rest your knife on the top right of your plate (diagonally), if you have switched hands to the American style to eat. Then simply put the fork down if you need a break.

4:20 pm Rule
Place your fork and knife together on the plate in a 4:20 pm position to say "I am finished." The knife's blade (sharp side) should face inward and fork prongs can either be up or down.

American Style in Action

Step 1. Criss-Cross
Cut the food using a criss-cross motion. Back and forth. Back and forth.

Step 2. Pass
Switch hands! Place the fork in the right hand and leave the knife on the corner of the plate while you eat.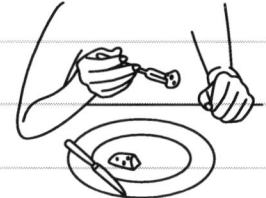

Step 3. Touch Down
Time to eat!

Step 4. Time Out
Time to let your fork and knife rest while you talk to your friend.

Step 5. Play is Complete
The meal is finished. Use the secret 4:20 pm code to let everyone know you are done!

Continental Style in Action

Step 1. Zig Zag & Score
Cut the food and begin eating. Do not switch hands.

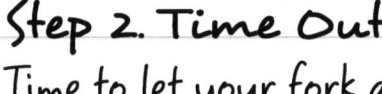
Step 2. Time Out
Time to let your fork and knife rest while you talk to your friend.

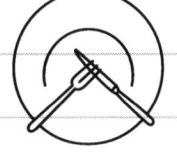
Step 3. Play is Complete
The meal is finished. Use the secret 4:20 pm code to let everyone know you are done!

Passing & Serving

Imagine driving a car on a race track. Pass the food in one direction so that dishes don't collide. The whole dish or entire bread basket should be passed. Don't throw a piece of bread across the table like a football. Traditionally the food is passed to the right. One person can also hold the dish so that the next person can take the food. Or he can just hand it to a person who then serves herself. Please don't drive the wrong way around the table!

> PASS THE WHOLE DISH IN ONE DIRECTION.

Bread & Butter

Bread is placed on the bread plate (if you have one) or on the side of your plate if you don't have one. Break off a small piece and eat one bite at a time. Don't take the whole piece of bread up to your mouth and bite off pieces. After all, we aren't dogs, trying to chew off the meat from a large bone, right?

> BREAK THE BREAD AND EAT ONE BITE AT A TIME.

How do you butter your bread? Rest the piece of bread against your plate and butter it. Butter one piece at a time.

RULE BREAKER!

✣ Don't take the last piece of bread without first offering it to others.

✣ Don't butter the whole bread and then take bites from it.

GAME CHALLENGE #4: Which statement is NOT true?

1 There are no rules for passing and serving food.
2 Bread should be placed on the bread plate.
3 Pass the whole dish in one direction.

Water Break

Imagine a big glass of juice sitting in front of you. Now you happen to be very hungry and thirsty. You stuff a large piece of chicken into your mouth and grab the milk to wash it down. STOP! Drinking and eating should be done separately. First chew and swallow the food. Then take a water break, making sure not to slurp or blow bubbles. Don't fill your cup so that it almost over flows. If you have a tickle or are choking, you might need a little sip of water to wash it down-a game exception!

> DRINKING AND EATING SHOULD BE DONE SEPARATELY.

Finished

In sports, everyone runs at different speeds. The same is true when we eat. When you are on the bench, you still stay and support the team. At a meal, wait until everyone is finished and then ask to be excused. Thank your mom or host for a delicious dinner! What happens after you finish playing a tennis game? Do you just stand up and leave without cleaning up the court? When you are done with dinner, offer to help clean up the kitchen!

> AT THE END OF A MEAL, THANK THE HOST AND ASK TO BE EXCUSED. OFFER TO HELP CLEAN UP.

GAME CHALLENGE #5: Name one good trick to use when setting the table?

Game Plan #2 - Mealtime Manners

1. Arrange flatware around the plate in the order that it is used.
2. Everything revolves around the main plate - MP.
3. Table setting tricks: 1. b and d rule, 2. Whose team are you on? 3. The word FORKS (minus the R).
4. Before you eat, wash your hands and dress appropriately.
5. Wait until everyone is seated. And follow your host.
6. Sit still. Use good posture and no elbows on the table.
7. Place the napkin in your lap and dab it on any stray bits of food.
8. When using utensils, follow the outside-in-rule: Use outside utensils first then work your way inward.
9. Hold the knife and fork correctly to cut and eat with ease.
10. Choose your eating style: American or Continental?
11. The secret codes of resting and finished positions - The backward "V", Time Out and 4:20 pm rule.
12. Pass the whole dish in one direction.
13. Break the bread and eat one bite at a time.
14. Drinking and eating should be done separately.
15. At the end of a meal, thank the host and ask to be excused. Offer to help clean up.

S M A R T

LET'S PRACTICE!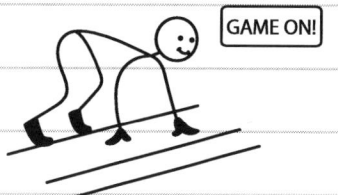

SECTION 1. You make the call!

Choose DO or DON'T. Complete this section and earn 10 tickets!

1. _____ Eat and drink at the same time.
2. _____ Chew with your mouth open.
3. _____ Put elbows on the table.
4. _____ Wipe your mouth with the corners of your napkin.
5. _____ Sit up straight while eating.
6. _____ Eat and talk at the same time.
7. _____ Place your silverware on the table after use.
8. _____ Make loud noises while eating.
9. _____ Place your napkin in your lap before eating.
10. _____ Comb your hair at the table.
11. _____ Play video games at the table while eating.
12. _____ Get up from the table whenever you feel bored.
13. _____ Use any utensil in any order during each meal.
14. _____ Passing the food to the right or left is fine as long as you follow the same direction as everyone.
15. _____ Take food from your friend's plate.
16. _____ Pick food out of your teeth with your hands.
17. _____ Use your fingers as a knife to help push up those little pieces of rice.
18. _____ Hold your fork with a clenched fist because it feels comfortable.
19. _____ Scrape the fork or spoon against your teeth.
20. _____ Place your napkin on the table during dinner.

SECTION 2. Can you make the free throw? - Earn 10 tickets! ☺

1. You are eating at your friend's house for dinner. His mom lets you know that dinner is ready. What should you do?
    a. Just pick a seat.
    b. Wait for your friend or his mom to show you where to sit.
    c. Sit wherever there is an open spot.
    d. Take the usual spot that you always have at home.

2. What should you do when you first sit down at the table?
    a. Begin serving whatever food is close to you.
    b. Start a conversation.
    c. Tuck your napkin under your chin.
    d. Watch what the hostess does.

3. Mrs. Lee bows her head and says a prayer after she sits down.
    a. Just start eating.
    b. Bow your head and wait quietly.
    c. Stare at everyone.

4. You have just finished your pasta but you would like more because it was delicious! Your mom has more pasta on a serving plate. How can you get more food?
    a. Mom, will you please give me more pasta?
    b. Mom, may I please have more pasta?
    c. Can I have some more pasta?

5. Your friend comes over for dinner and begins playing with her food. She also decides to burp. What should you do?
    a. Begin playing with your food too. It looks like fun!

      b. Ignore her and keep eating politely.

      c. Tell her to stop because she is being very rude!

6. You are asked to pass the food. What should you do?
   - a. Pass the food to the right.
   - b. Pass it to whoever is hungry.
   - c. Pass it to the left.
   - d. Throw it across the table.

7. Your friend would like a bread roll. Just hand him a piece.
   - a. True
   - b. False

8. Circle all the correct statements about using a napkin.
   - a. Leave it alongside your plate so that you can see it.
   - b. Open it up when you sit down and place it on your lap.
   - c. Leave it on your chair when you are finished.
   - d. When finished place the napkin on your plate.
   - e. Tuck it under your chin.

9. Your nose starts to run during dinner. Now what should you do?
   - a. Just take your napkin and give it a good blow and wipe.
   - b. Dab your nose very discreetly and then excuse yourself to go to the bathroom.
   - c. Wipe your nose with your shirt sleeve.

10. What do you do if you have just taken a big bite of your food and someone asks you a question?

      a. Talk with your mouth full.
      b. Chew and swallow before answering.
      c. Spit out your food.

11. You have just taken a bite out of your food and feel that the food is stuck in between your teeth. Now what do you do?
      a. Stick your hand in your mouth and grab out the piece of food.
      b. Use your fork to pick at your mouth.
      c. Discreetly use your tongue to dislodge the food from your tooth.
      d. Excuse yourself and use the bathroom.

12. You are really hungry and you can't seem to get the food onto your fork easily. What should you do?
      a. Use your fingers to place the food onto your fork.
      b. Use your fingers and stuff the food directly into your mouth.
      c. Use a knife to push the food onto the fork.

13. You have just taken a bite out of the chicken and realize that a piece of bone is in your mouth. Now what do you do?
      a. Spit it out on the plate and say EHHHHH!!!
      b. Announce to everyone that you have a piece of bone in your mouth.
      c. Discreetly use a napkin to quietly remove the piece of bone.

14. You just drank a big glass of soda and now feel the need to burp.
      a. Give a loud burp.
      b. Cover your mouth with a napkin and keep your mouth closed to cover up any noise.
      c. Excuse yourself and go to the bathroom.

15. You have just finished eating your dinner and would like to get up and go outside. It's a beautiful day and playing outside is so much fun! What should you do?
    a. Get up and run outdoors without asking for permission and without helping with the dishes.
    b. Ask to be excused and help with the dishes quickly so that you have time to play.
    c. Ask to be excused.

16. When you are eating a piece of chicken how do you cut it?
    a. One or two pieces as you eat it.
    b. All of it before you begin.
    c. Half of it to begin with.

17. You sit down at a formal table setting and they have 3 forks placed. What should you do?
    a. Use the one you are the most comfortable with.
    b. Use the fork closest to the plate.
    c. Ask the host or waiter why you have 3 forks.
    d. Use the one farthest from your plate first.

18. You are eating dinner at a friend's house and you find a piece of hair in the food. What should you do?
    a. Yell out 'EWWW! Is that a piece of hair in my food?"
    b. Discreetly eat around the food that has the piece of hair.
    c. Eat the piece of hair. It's just a piece of hair; the food is still pretty good!

SECTION 3. Scrimmage!

Recruit family and friends to play these games.
Each game is worth one ticket. The more times you play, the more you earn.

Manners and Candies - Practice 10 different table rules:
- Rule #1 - Place the napkin on your lap
- Rule #2 - Use your utensils, NOT your fingers!
- Rule #3 - No reaching
- Rule #4 - Don't start eating until the cook is seated.
- Rule #5 - No bodily noises (slurping, burping, chewing with your mouth open, smacking your lips, etc.)
- Rule #6 - Don't leave the table until everyone has finished eating.
- Rule #7 - No elbows on the table.
- Rule #8 - No rude comments about the food.
- Rule #9 - Sit up straight and don't tip your chair.
- Rule #10 - Everyone stays to clean up the dishes and the mess!

Everyone gets a little teaser bowl or bag with small candies like M & Ms or Skittles. This will be the delicious dessert! Now the better you behave, the better chance you have to keep your dessert. Everyone has to keep an eye out to see if anyone is breaking the rules. If you break any rule you have to give a piece to the person who called you out. How much candy will you get to keep?

Fancy Dinner! - The whole family pretends that we are at a restaurant and are about to eat a formal dinner. In a sophisticated setting, we need to be dressed for the occasion and use perfect manners. Use candles and dim the lights. Make it extra special!

Set the Table Challenge - Who can set the table with all the dishes and utensils in the right place?

Secret Manner Agent - One person is assigned to be the Secret Manner Agent for the night. The secret agent will award a special dessert to the person who showed off great manner skills.

SECTION 4. Mealtime Crossword Puzzle - Earn 5 tickets! ☺

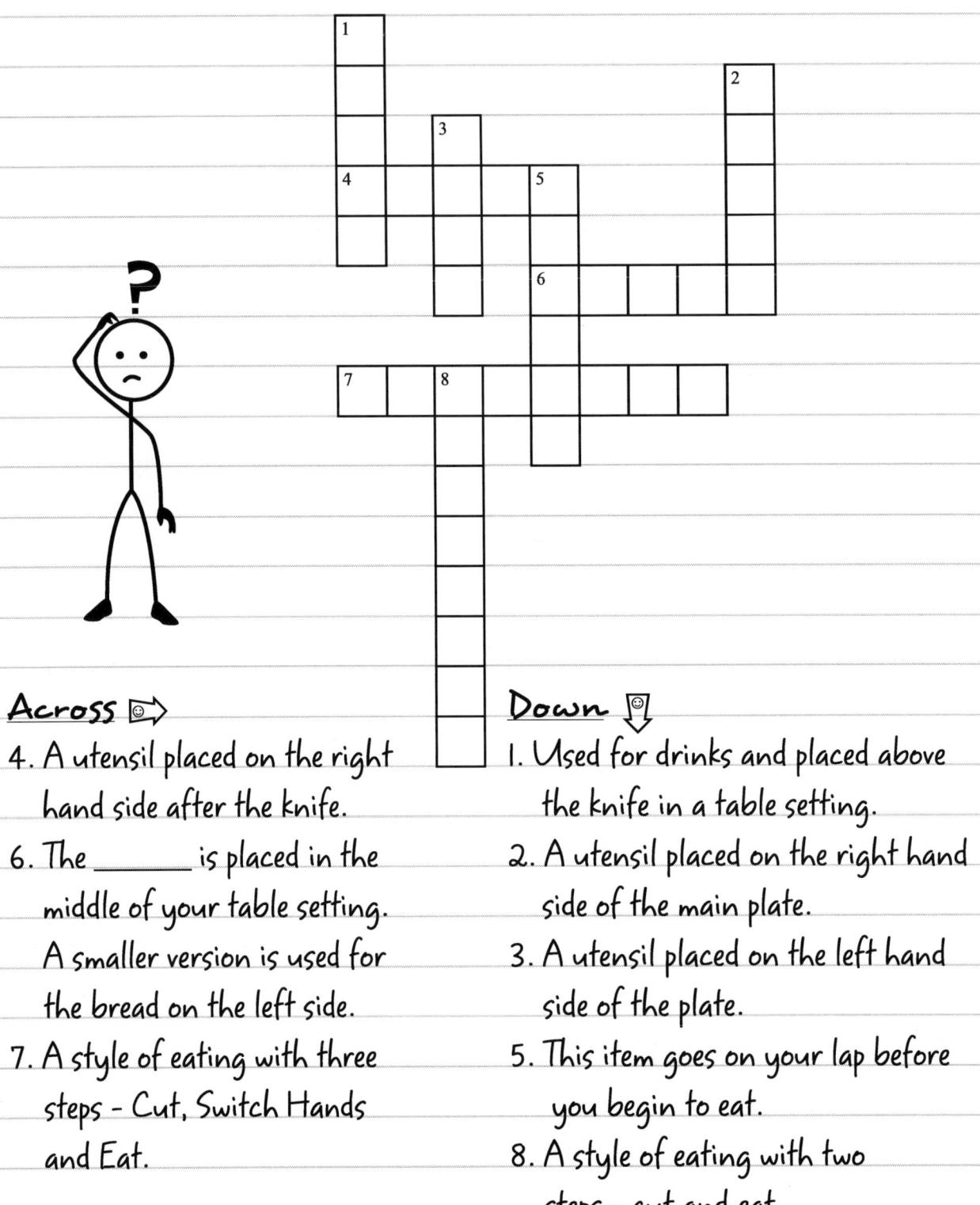

Across ➡
4. A utensil placed on the right hand side after the knife.
6. The _____ is placed in the middle of your table setting. A smaller version is used for the bread on the left side.
7. A style of eating with three steps - Cut, Switch Hands and Eat.

Down ⬇
1. Used for drinks and placed above the knife in a table setting.
2. A utensil placed on the right hand side of the main plate.
3. A utensil placed on the left hand side of the plate.
5. This item goes on your lap before you begin to eat.
8. A style of eating with two steps - cut and eat.

Words to Play: Plate, Knife, Fork, Spoon, Glass, American, European, Napkin

SECTION 5. Mealtime Manners Word Search – Earn 5 tickets! ☺

```
R W C N Z U O W K S E N Y L Z
T F O D Y Y W F G F M M G M N
B L N O E Q S O C T I P Q Z W
D P T N Q H R X B E T M M O D
N T I V G G S M G E L B A T Q
M F N W K I L I A V A Y Q U S
X H E A J A S M N U E K Z L K
M Z N I V J E V D I M K I S N
D X T J R R Y U A E F S P F I
K Z A P I W B Z N V N O K R F
R J L C M V B G K E O N P Q E
O N A P K I N R T N F L B T Q
F N A C S B L U E B E S E U L
R P C C J K A Q G A U Z P Y F
G N I K N I R D S S D Z G O Q
```

AMERICAN	BREAD
CONTINENTAL	DRINKING
FINISHED	FORK
KNIFE	MEALTIME
NAPKIN	SPOON
TABLE	UTENSILS
VSIGN	

ANSWERS

Game Challenges:

#1) 1. Knife should be next to the plate on the right. 2. Bread plate should be diagonally top left from MP. 3. Napkin should be on the left side. 4. Soup spoon is to the right of the knife. 5. Water cup should be on the right hand side above the knife.

Formal table setting: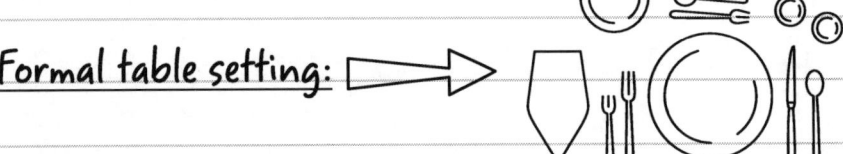

#2) True

#3) If you have a choice of two forks, you should use the fork on the outside first for the appetizer. The second fork closest to the plate is the entrée fork.

#4) 1 - There are no rules for passing and serving food.

#5) Letters b and d. Whose team are you on? The word FORKS!

Game On:

SECTION 1. You make the call!

1. Don't, 2. Don't, 3. Don't, 4. Do, 5. Do, 6. Don't, 7. Don't, 8. Don't, 9. Do, 10. Don't, 11. Don't, 12. Don't, 13. Don't, 14. Do, 15. Don't, 16. Don't, 17. Don't, 18. Don't, 19. Don't, 20. Don't.

SECTION 2. Can you make the free throw?

1. b, 2. b and/or d, 3. b, 4. b, 5. b, 6. a, 7. b. Pass the bread basket, 8. b and d, 9. b, 10. b, 11. c or d, 12. c, 13. c, 14. b or c, 15. b, 16. a, 17. d, 18. b

SECTION 3. Scrimmage!

Answers will vary. Please discuss answers with your coach (an adult).

SECTION 4. Word Search

```
+ + C + + + + + + E + + + +
+ + O D + + + + + M + + + +
+ + N + E + + + + I + + + +
+ + T N + H + + + T + + + +
+ + I + G + S + + E L B A T +
+ + N + + I + I A + A + + + S
+ + E + + + S M N + E + + L K
+ + N + + + E V + I M + I S N
+ + T + + R + + + + F S P + I
K + A + I + + + + N O + + F
R + L C + + B + + E O + + + E
O N A P K I N R T N + + + + +
F N + + + + + U E + + + + + +
+ + + + + + + + A + + + + +
G N I K N I R D + + D + + + +
```

(Over, Down, Direction)
AMERICAN(9,6,SW)
BREAD(7,11,SE)
CONTINENTAL(3,1,S)
DRINKING(8,15,W)
FINISHED(11,9,NW)
FORK(1,13,N)
KNIFE(15,7,S)
MEALTIME(11,8,N)
NAPKIN(2,12,E)
SPOON(14,8,SW)
TABLE(14,5,W)
UTENSILS(8,13,NE)
VSIGN(8,8,NW)

SECTION 5. Crossword Puzzle

Across ➡ 4. Spoon   6. Plate   7. American

Down ⬇ 1. Glass   2. Knife   3. Fork   5. Napkin   8. European

SMART
Ticket Tally Score Board

Ask an adult to place a check on a ticket after each game challenge or practice section. How many tickets were you able to collect?

Notes:

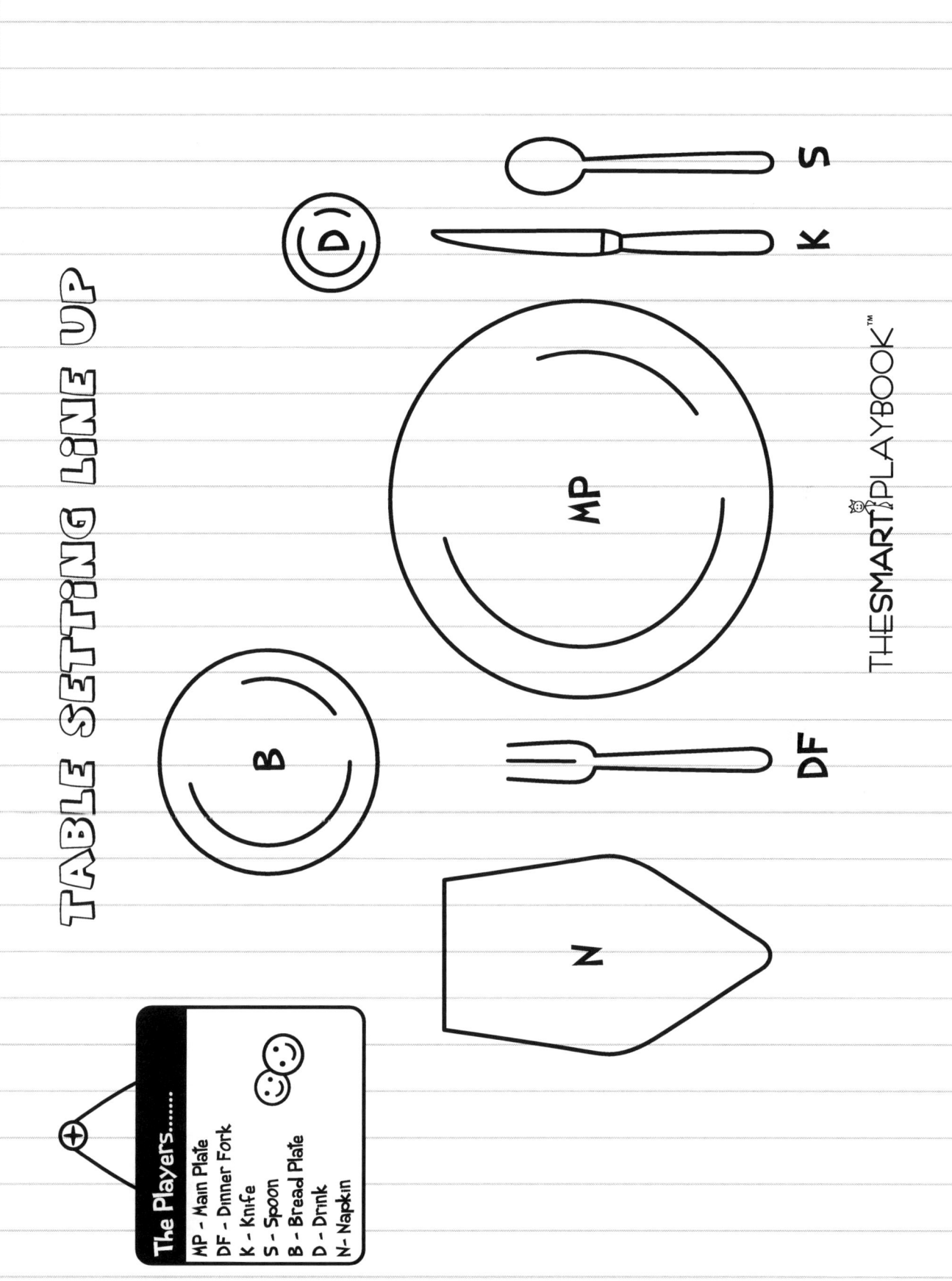

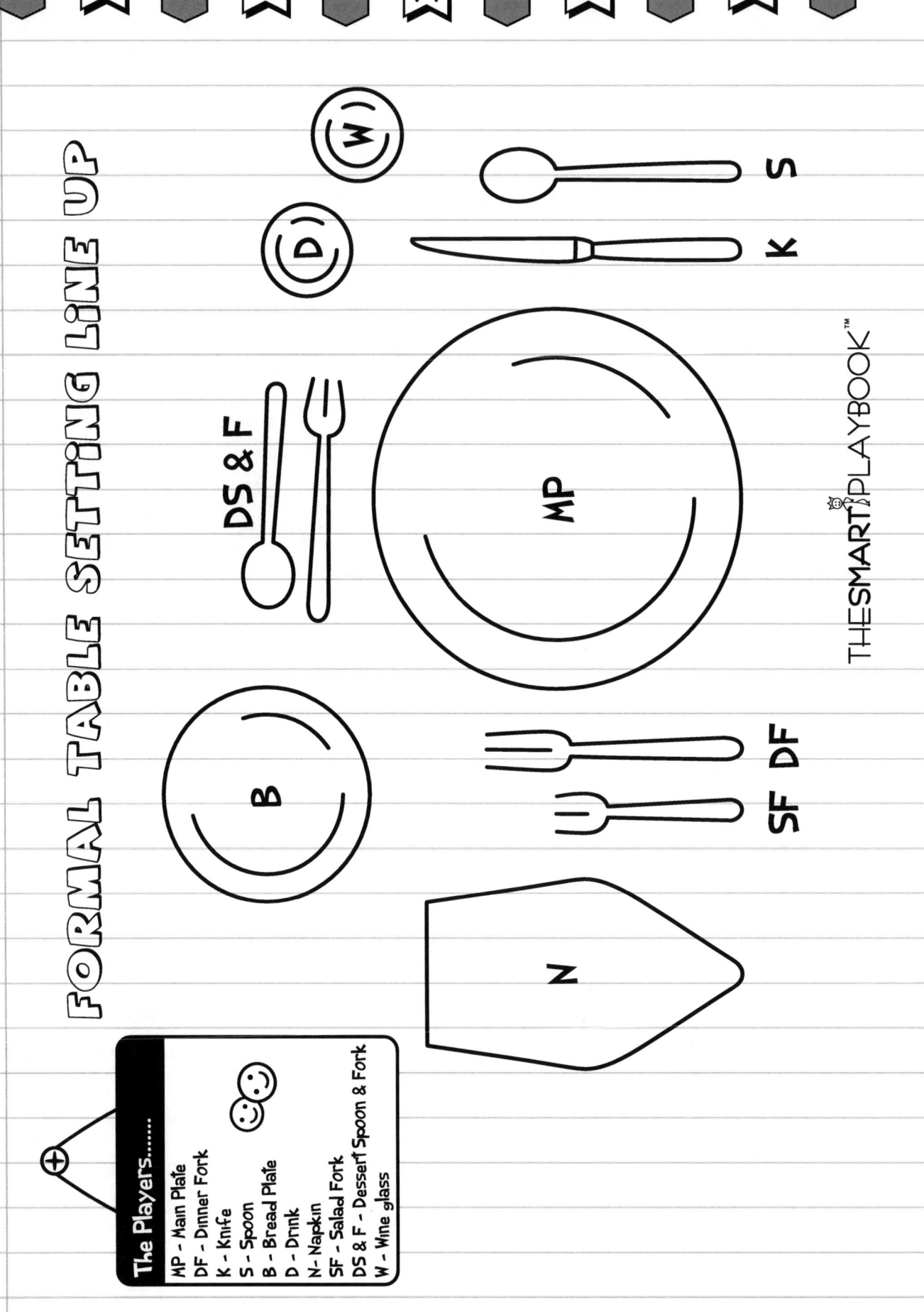

SMART
DECODE THE DRESS CODE

Match your look with the place or situation

INFORMAL - Come as you are!

Jeans, Shorts, Pants, Sweatpants, Skirt, Casual Dress, T-Shirt, Sweatshirt, Long Sleeve Shirt, Collared Shirt, Sweater, Polo Shirt, Athletic Uniform, Casual Shoes

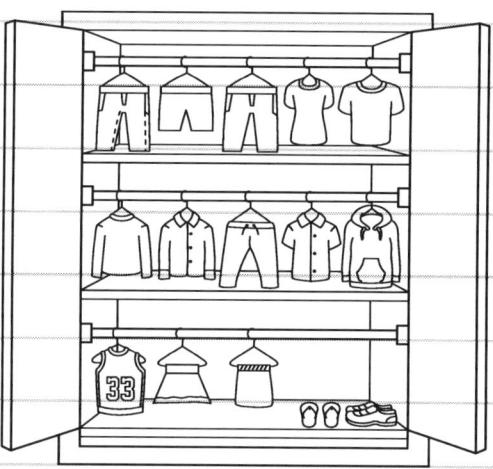

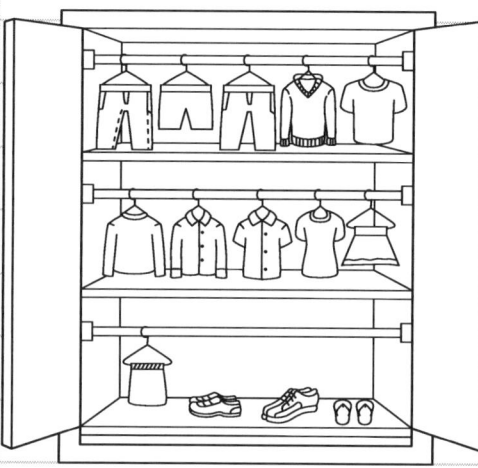

CASUAL - Comfortable yet presentable!

Jeans, Shorts, Pants, Skirt, Casual Dress, T-Shirt, Sweatshirt, Long Sleeve Shirt, Sweater, Collared Shirt, Polo shirt, Casual Shoes

CASUAL ELEGANT - Dress to impress!

Dress Pants, Dress Sweater, Party Dress or Skirt, Sweater Vest, Polo Shirt, Blazer, Dress Shirt, More Formal Shoes

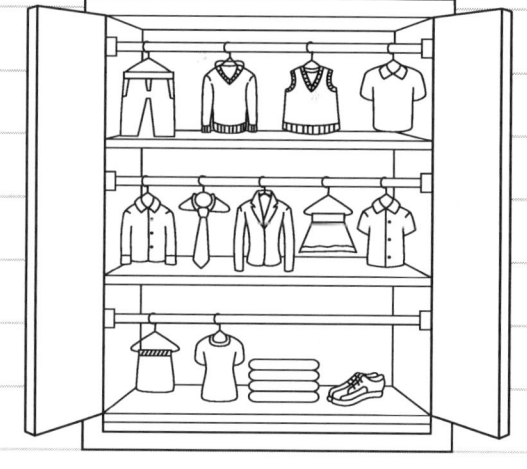

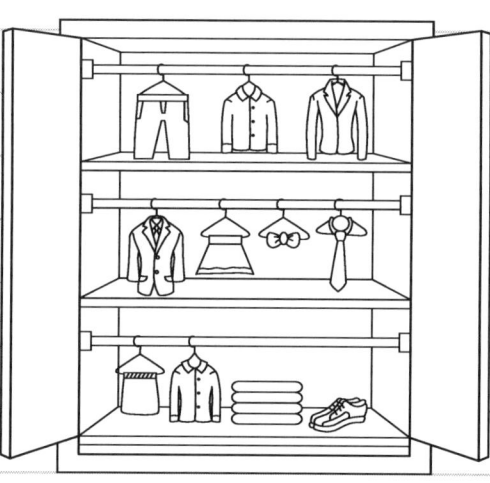

FORMAL - Dress to impress to the max!

Formal Pants & Shirts, Your Nicest Party Skirt or Dress, Blazer, Suit, Formal Shoes (When in doubt ask an adult for help!)

THE SMART PLAYBOOK™

**Copyrighted Material

SMART
DIY CONVERSATION CARDS

Perk up your family talk! Just cut out the cards. Create the family talk jar. One person picks a card and everyone can answer the same question or everyone can pick their own. Listen and take turns.

SEASONS OF THE YEAR
What is your favorite season? Why? Do you know an interesting fact about your favorite season? Name a fun family activity during this season?

FAVORITE SPORTS
What is your favorite sport? Who is your favorite player? Who is your favorite team? What's an interesting fact?

PLAN A DREAM VACATION
Where would you go on a dream vacation? Who would come? What would you do? Why? What's an interesting fact about your choice?

FAVORITE CANDY
What type of candy do you like to eat? What would happen if you ate tons of candy every day?

EXERCISE IMPORTANT
Why should we exercise? What are some forms of exercising? How many times a week should we exercise? What is your favorite type of exercise? What is your least favorite exercise?

SUPERPOWERS
If you could have any superpower, which would you choose? Why?

ANIMAL
If you could be an animal, what would you be and why?

YOUR FAVORITE THING
What is one thing you couldn't live without? Why?

FAME FOR 10 SECONDS
If you had the attention of the world for 10 seconds, what would you say? Why?

BEST HOLIDAY
What is your favorite holiday to celebrate? Why?

INTERESTING FACTS ABOUT YOU
Name three interesting things about you?

TEACH A CLASS FOR A DAY
If you had to teach a class for a day, what subject would you choose? What would you do?

THE SMART PLAYBOOK™

**Copyrighted Material

SMART
THANK YOU DRILL

Follow the guide and add your creative play! Fill in the name and replace the number with words. Use the list or come up with something original!

#1

awesome gift

cool present

perfect gift

thoughtful gift

fun gift

yummy cake

_____ (name of the gift)

_____ (be creative!)

#2

play with it

use it

try it

test it out

eat it

_____ (something original)

#3

Mention the gift again. Here you can choose something from list #1 again.

Dear _____Name_____.

Thank you so much for the _____1_____.

I love it! I can't wait to _____2_____.

That was very kind of you to remember me.

Thanks again for _____3_____.

Hope to see you soon.

Sincerely,

_____

2-POINT CONVERSION TO TOP IT OFF:

Score bonus points and add a little extra to your card....

- A photo of you playing with your new toy
- Bake something to bring with your card
- A drawing

A MORE CREATIVE PLAY:

A techy modern thank you!

Use the smartphone to create a unique thank you with your own words and personality.

- Create a picture with captions
- A video that captures your excitement opening the gift and how grateful you are!
- Send a picture by email or text of you wearing the new coat holding up a thank you sign
- Create a video of yourself playing soccer with the new ball

THE SMART PLAYBOOK™

**Copyrighted Material

SMART
TECH CODE OF CONDUCT

I promise to use all technology responsibly. This includes cell phone, computer, tablet, Xbox, Wii, iPods and any website that I visit or join. Please check the following statements to show that you have read them and understand them:

- ☐ I will not give away personal information such as my address, phone number, school information without my parent's consent.
- ☐ I will not befriend people that I have not met in real life without my parent's consent.
- ☐ I will never say anything unkind toward anyone for any reason on the internet.
- ☐ If I see someone being mean to another person, I will tell them to stop and then tell my parents.
- ☐ If someone is mean to me online I will not respond. I will instead tell my parents.
- ☐ I am not allowed to lie about my age to join any website or to use an app.
- ☐ I will stay courteous, respectful and considerate while using all technology.
- ☐ I will never forward any photos or information written by someone else without their permission.
- ☐ I will never share photos where I am posing in a way that I wouldn't in front of my parents.
- ☐ I will not download music, games or software without my parent's consent.
- ☐ I will never use inappropriate language online.
- ☐ I will immediately close any pop-up boxes with the x button.
- ☐ I understand that people are not always who they say they are, not everyone tells the truth and there is no such thing as privacy online.
- ☐ I will not sign up for anything online without my parent's consent
- ☐ I will always tell my parents if something makes me uncomfortable on the internet - an email, a website etc.
- ☐ I will take care of all my technology gadgets and remember that they are expensive.

_____   _____
Player Signature   Coach Signature

**Copyrighted Material

The SMART Playbook is available at www.thesmartplaybook.com. Buy as one complete book with all five game plans (Best Value!) or by topic. Tailor your game plan to your family needs!

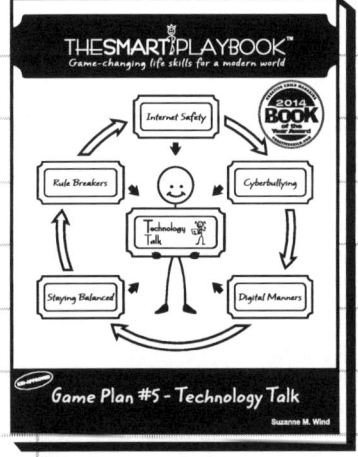
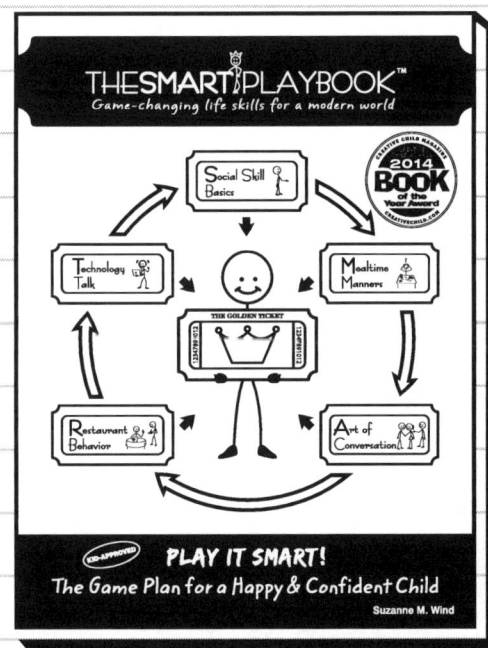

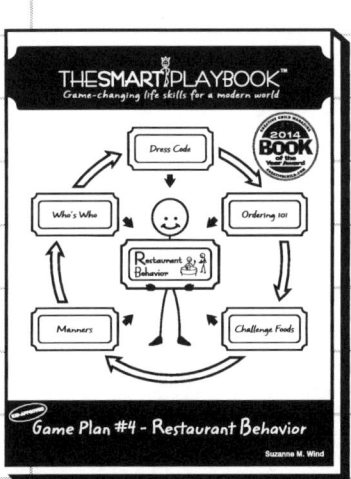

Made in the USA
Lexington, KY
17 April 2017